DATE DUE

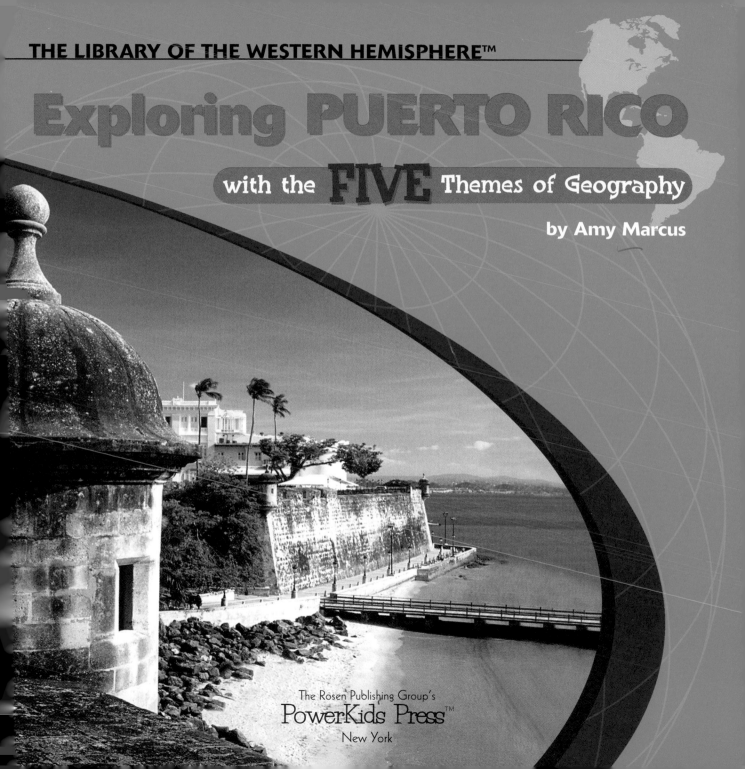

Exploring PUERTO RICO

with the FIVE Themes of Geography

by Amy Marcus

The Rosen Publishing Group's

PowerKids Press™

New York

Published in 2005 by The Rosen Publishing Group, Inc.
29 East 21st Street, New York, NY 10010

First Edition

Editor: Geeta Sobha
Book Design: Michelle Innes

Photo Credits: Cover, p. 1 © Steve Dunwell/Getty Images; pp. 9, 21 (national forest) © Wolfgang Kaehler/Corbis; p. 9 (Isla Palamino) © Jean du Boisberranger/Getty Images; p. 9 (Rio Camuy Cave Park) © David Boyer/National Geographic Image Collection; p. 10 © Bettman/Corbis; pp. 10 (parrot), 11 © Kevin Schafer/Corbis; p. 12 © Robert Frerck/Panoramic Images/NGSImages.com; p. 12 (mall) © Macduff Everton/Corbis; p. 15 © Bill Ross/Corbis; p. 15 (tropical fruit farm) © Tom Bean/Corbis; p. 16 © Rob Badger/Getty Images; p. 16 (hurricane damage) © Tony Arruza/Corbis; p. 19 © Andrea Pistolesi/Getty Images; p. 19 (Tren Urbano) © David Sailors/Corbis; p. 19 (Tito Puente) © Mitchell Gerber/Corbis; p. 21 (Ponce) © Neil Rabinowitz/Corbis

Library of Congress Cataloging-in-Publication Data

Marcus, Amy.
    Exploring Puerto Rico with the five themes of geography / by Amy Marcus. — 1st ed.
    p. cm. — (The library of the Western Hemisphere)
    ISBN 1-4042-2673-7 (lib. bdg.) — ISBN 0-8239-4633-9 (pbk.)
    1. Puerto Rico—Geography—Juvenile literature. [1. Puerto Rico—Geography.] I.
    Title.   II. Series.

F1958.M37 2005
917.295—dc22

                                                            2003025741

Contents

The FIVE Themes of Geography

Geography is the study of Earth, including its climate, resources, physical features, and people. To study a particular country or area, such as Puerto Rico, geographers use the five themes of geography: location, place, human-environment interaction, movement, and regions. These themes help us organize and understand important information about the geography of places around the world. Let's use the five themes to find out more about Puerto Rico.

1 Location

Where is Puerto Rico?

We can define where Puerto Rico is by using its absolute, or exact, location. Absolute location tells exactly where a place is in the world. The imaginary lines of longitude and latitude are used to define absolute location.

We can also define a place by using its relative, or general, location, which tells where a place is in relation to other places nearby. What countries is it near? Is it bordered by bodies of water? Relative location can also be described by using cardinal directions: east, west, north, and south.

2 Place

What is Puerto Rico like?

To know Puerto Rico, we can study its physical and human features. Physical features include landforms, bodies of water, natural resources, climate, and plant and animal life. Human features are things that have been created by people. Buildings, cities, government, and traditions are examples of human features.

3 Human-Environment Interaction

How do the people and the environment of Puerto Rico affect each other?

Human-environment interaction explains how the land has affected the way people in Puerto Rico live. It also explains how the people have changed their environment or adapted to it.

4 Movement

How do people, goods, and ideas get from place to place in Puerto Rico?

This theme explains how products, people, and ideas move around the country. It can also show how they move from Puerto Rico to other places.

5 Regions

What does Puerto Rico have in common with other places around the world? How are places within Puerto Rico grouped?

Places are grouped into regions by physical and human features that they share. This theme studies the features that Puerto Rico shares with other areas, making it part of a certain region. It looks at political and physical regions within Puerto Rico.

Puerto Rico's absolute location is 18° north and 66° west. Puerto Rico's relative location can be defined by looking at the places that surround it. The island of Puerto Rico is located in the Caribbean Sea. Puerto Rico is 1,000 miles (1,609 kilometers) southeast of Florida. It is located between the U.S. Virgin Islands and the island of Hispaniola, on which the Dominican Republic and Haiti are located.

Where in the World?

Absolute location is the point where the lines of longitude and latitude meet.

Longitude tells a place's position in degrees east or west of the prime meridian, a line that runs through Greenwich, London.

Latitude tells a place's position in degrees north or south of the equator, the imaginary line that goes around the middle of the earth.

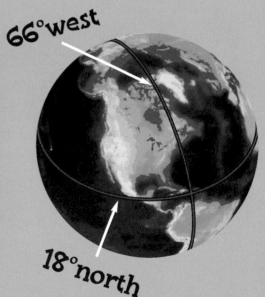

66°west

18°north

Culebra, Vieques, and Mona Island are all part of Puerto Rico. The city of San Juan is the capital of Puerto Rico.

Atlantic Ocean

Hispaniola

Dominican Republic

San Juan

Culebra

Puerto Rico

Mona Island

Vieques

Virgin Islands

Caribbean Sea

Physical Features

Puerto Rico has three main geographic areas: the interior mountains, the coastal lowlands, and the karst region. The coastal lowlands are on the north and south coasts of the island. The northern coast has a humid climate. The southern lowlands are much drier than the northern coast.

Northwestern Puerto Rico is known as the karst region. This region was formed when limestone was worn away by rain. This left large holes in the ground, called sinkholes. Beneath the sinkholes lie endless caves and tunnels.

About three-fourths of Puerto Rico is covered by hills and mountains. The Cordillera Central is a mountain range that goes across the island, from east to west. The Caribbean National Forest is in La Sierra de Luquillo mountain range. This area gets more than 100 inches (254 centimeters) of rain per year and has a tropical climate.

Several small islands, such as Isla Palomino, belong to Puerto Rico. Isla Palomino is made up of coral.

Rio Camuy Cave Park is located in Puerto Rico's karst region. It is the third largest cave system in the world.

The Caribbean National Forest, Puerto Rico's rain forest, gets about 120 inches (304 centimeters) of rain a year.

The royal poinciana tree is also called the flamboyant tree or the peacock tree. It can grow to be 20 to 40 feet (6 to 12 meters) high.

The Puerto Rican parrot is in danger of disappearing from the wild. It can only be found in a few parts of the Caribbean National Forest.

The climate of Puerto Rico is warm and sunny. The average temperature is about 73°F (23° C) in January and 80°F (27° C) in July. Even the water surrounding Puerto Rico is warm. It's usually about 80°F (27° C) year round. Though rain falls throughout the year, the rainiest months are from May to December.

Thousands of varieties of tropical plants grow in Puerto Rico, including kapok trees, the colorful poinciana, and the coconut palm.

Puerto Rico's wildlife includes iguanas, small lizards, and many types of bats. There are also birds such as nightingales and gorriones.

The coqui is a tiny frog that gets its name from the chirping sound it makes.

Malls in Puerto Rico have many U.S. chain stores, restaurants, and movie theaters.

El Morro is a fort that was built by the Spanish to protect San Juan.

Human Features

Almost 3,900,000 people live on the island of Puerto Rico. Both Spanish and English are the official languages of Puerto Rico. This is because Puerto Rico was a colony of Spain. In 1898, Puerto Rico was taken over by the United States. Puerto Rico is a commonwealth of the United States. Puerto Ricans do not pay federal income tax, and they cannot vote in presidential elections. Puerto Rico has its own government, led by a governor.

The influence of Spanish and American cultures can be seen throughout Puerto Rico. On the island, you can see traditional Spanish-style architecture in buildings such as La Fortaleza, which was built in 1533. Latin music, such as salsa, merengue, and bomba, as well as rock and rap music are popular.

About one-third of the people of Puerto Rico live in and around San Juan, the island's capital. San Juan is found on the northern coast. Most of Puerto Rico's population live and work along the northern coast.

Farmers in Puerto Rico grow coffee beans, pineapples, and mangoes. Dairy products have become important to the country's economy. Puerto Ricans take advantage of natural resources such as limestone, clay, cobalt, chromium, nickel, iron ore, and copper.

Puerto Ricans rely on the beauty of their country as a resource. Tourists come from all over the world to visit Puerto Rico's beaches and rain forests.

Over the last 60 years, production of glass, leather, rubber, and plastic have become important businesses. However, as the number of factories grew in Puerto Rico,

Farmers in Puerto Rico grow tropical fruits to sell to other countries.

Because of the great number of tourists, many hotels have been built in San Juan.

Hurricanes can cause millions of dollars in damage to land and property.

Pollution from gold mines can damage forests and rivers.

so did the pollution of the country's environment. Oil and chemical plants polluted the water, killing fish and forcing Puerto Rico to import many types of food. Also, the island of Vieques has been polluted by equipment used by the U.S. Navy. The U.S. Navy occupied Vieques for about 60 years.

Puerto Rico has no natural lakes. Several man-made lakes were formed when dams were built across rivers. These dams are used to provide water for hydroelectricity and irrigation.

Puerto Rico can be struck by fierce hurricanes, especially from August to October. However, they do not affect where people choose to live. Puerto Ricans have found ways to protect their houses. The houses are built of concrete to protect them from the severe winds.

4 Movement

People and information move in and out of Puerto Rico in many ways. Luis Muñoz Marín International Airport is one of the largest and busiest airports in the country. Ports in San Juan are stopping places for ships going across the Atlantic Ocean.

There are over 14,000 miles (22,531 km) of roads in Puerto Rico. These provide transportation routes for people and supplies across the island. A new transportation system, Tren Urbano, is currently under construction. Tren Urbano is a light-rail system that will serve the major cities on the island.

Several newspapers are published in Puerto Rico, including *El Nuevo Día* and *El Vocero de Puerto Rico*. There are about 20 television stations and 90 radio stations.

Puerto Rican writers such as Enrique Laguerre have gained worldwide recognition.

Musicians, such as Tito Puente, have taken Latin music to the world outside of Puerto Rico.

The Tren Urbano will run through San Juan, easing the traffic flow of the highly populated area.

Cruise ships bring tourists into ports in San Juan.

Puerto Rico is part of many different regions. Politically, it is a commonwealth of the United States. Puerto Rico is divided into 78 *municipios*, or municipalities. Each *municipio* is governed by a mayor.

Geographically, Puerto Rico is part of the West Indies. The West Indies is an archipelago, or a chain of islands, that stretches from south of Florida to the northern coast of South America.

Puerto Rico is part of a cultural region called Latin America, where most people speak a Romance language, such as Spanish, Portuguese, or French. Latin America is made up of the countries in the Western Hemisphere south of the United States, including the West Indies.

The Caribbean National Forest, also called El Yunque, is located in the northeastern part of Puerto Rico.

Atlantic Ocean

Rio de la Plata

Karst Region

El Yunque

Cordillera Central

Ponce

Ponce is Puerto Rico's second largest city. It is located in the south of Puerto Rico.

Caribbean Sea

21

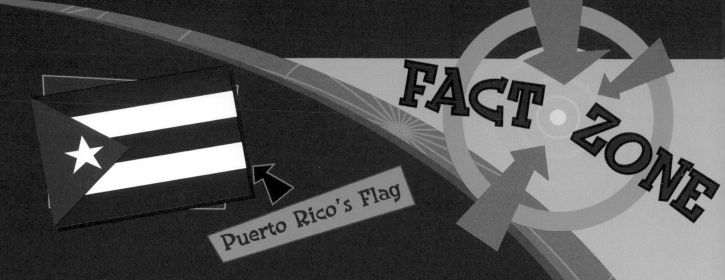

Puerto Rico's Flag

Population (2003) 3,885,877

Languages Spanish and English

Absolute location 18° north, 66° west

Capital city San Juan

Area 3,515 square miles (9,104 square kilometers)

Highest point Cerro de Punta 4,389 feet (1,338 meters)

Lowest point Caribbean coast zero feet

Land boundaries none

Natural resources copper and nickel

Agricultural products sugarcane, coffee, pineapples, plantains, bananas, livestock products, and chickens

Major exports chemicals, electronics, apparel, canned tuna, rum, beverage concentrates, and medical equipment

Major imports chemicals, electrical machinery, transportation equipment, clothing, food, fish, and petroleum products

Glossary

architecture (AR-ki-tek-chur) The style in which buildings are designed.

commonwealth (KOM-uhn-welth) A nation or state governed by the people living there.

culture (KUHL-chur) The way of life, ideas, customs, and traditions shared by a group of people.

humid (HYOO-mid) Damp and moist.

hydroelectricity (hye-droh-i-lek-TRISS-uh-tee) Electricity produced by water power that turns a generator.

interaction (in-tur-AK-shuhn) The action between people, groups, or things.

irrigation (IHR-uh-gay-shuhn) When water is applied to crops by using channels and pipes.

limestone (LIME-stohn) A rock formed from the remains of shells or coral.

region (REE-juhn) An area or a district.

resource (ri-SORSS) Something that is valuable or useful to a place or person.

tropical (TROP-uh-kuhl) To do with or living in the hot, rainy area of the earth.

Index

Web Sites

Due to the changing nature of Internet links, PowerKids Press has developed an on-line list of Web sites related to the subject of this book. This site is updated regularly. Please use this link to access the list:
http://www.powerkidslinks.com/lwh/puertori